Just Believe

Don't Perform

TROY BARNES

RIGHT SIDE
PUBLISHING

Just Believe, Don't Perform

TABLE OF CONTENTS

.

Introduction

Then they asked him, "What must we do to do the works God requires?"
Jesus answered, "The work of God is this: to believe in the one he has sent"

John 6:28 and 29

Published by Right side publishing

P.O 339 Reynoldsburg Ohio

rightsideceo@yahoo.com

Edited by: Sam Ikner, Felicia Cauley

Project manager-Robert Cauley

ISBN: 978-1-955050-91-3

LCCN: 2022908750

Chapter One:

Beacon of Hope

It was January 2018, and I had just moved into the church building that houses the Beacon for Him ministry outreach in downtown Long Beach California. The outreach is run by the president and founder Shannon James.

She was the one who, in my last book *Amazing Grace – My Journey into God's Unmerited Favor*, told me as I was getting ready to go home to Columbus Ohio for the Christmas holiday, "When you come back, I don't want you to go back to the mission (homeless shelter) I want you to stay here".

At that point I had been there around 5 days and was getting adjusted to not only not staying at the mission in a dorm with a lot of other guys, but now staying in a church building with 3 other guys. Each person had their own room, and Shannon graciously had a small closet cleaned out for me. The closet was just big enough to make a bedroom out of. I could hang up all my clothes and keep my personal belongings along with having a key to lock it when I wasn't there, or events would take place so no one else could get in. I can't even begin to tell you how grateful I was to be in this position with her help as well as the help of so many others around this time.

Beacon for Him was way more than an outreach ministry it was a FAMILY in every sense of the word. People that I worked with there and saw on a weekly basis I could pick out and tell you how I felt they related to me in the family sense. There was of course Shannon who was the sister I never had. Then there was Carol and Donna, who were like my favorite aunts.

Donna oversaw the handing out of clothes to those in need while Carol worked the kitchen. Carol and I along with Shannon would also plan nights out for the group at times, such as going bowling or out to dinner just to have fun. There was Johnny who was like a brother to me and was the leader of the Youth with A Mission (YWAM), whose ministry partnered with Beacon and was there to help at all events no matter where or what time. He and his team, his wife Nina, friends Jonik and Elyse (who were married), and another friend named Ben among others were always there to help. They even would invite me over for dinner every couple of weeks as part of their ministry get together group outings and fellowship.

I met a lot of people through them as well as at Beacon and was very grateful for all these new friendships. There were others that worked in and around the ministry volunteering like my brothers Hector, and John. Also, Sheila, her husband AL, and their friend Diane who were like my uncle and aunties.

I worked with them every Thursday for our food distribution efforts, packing and passing out groceries to those in need. They would also invite me out to eat, to get coffee or just for fellowship. Diane even took it a step further as someone who really helped me while staying at the mission.

Here I was, with all my clothes and some personal belongings that I could not keep at the shelter, so since she only lived a few blocks away she offered to allow me to house my extra stuff at her place. She had a big shed in her backyard, so I used it to keep some of my things.

Talk about a lifesaver, as these people I've mentioned were purposely positioned by God to help me, and I was positioned to be of help to them as well whenever needed. As I said in my previous book, it was all his Amazing Grace.

Chapter Two:

Just Believe, Don't Perform

So, 5 days into my stay at Beacon in January, it's an extremely bright sunny day in Southern California around noon, and I decided to go for a walk downtown. Maybe I'd get something to eat and just try to be content with the situation I was in, as I really had a lot to be thankful for.

As I open the front door, walk down the ramp in front of the building, turn to my left and take maybe 5 or 6 steps suddenly, the unthinkable happens, I'm grabbed on both sides of my arms by 2 very strong men. It happened so fast I could barely turn my head to see who it was and all I could hear them say in my ear is "DON'T MOVE"! Then as I'm trying to move, I heard again, "I SAID DON'T MOVE."

The next thing I know I'm up against a car in the parking lot beside Beacon and they are putting me in handcuffs. Needless to say, I thought I was going to lose all my bodily functions, I almost did. I really don't know how I stayed so composed unless it was fear that if I did anything I would get beaten just like Rodney King did in 1991, which was the first thing that crossed my mind. Once again, it was God's grace, but I remember I just started asking,

"What did I do? What's going on? You can't tell me what I did?" At that point, I heard, "Sir you're going to have to be patient, we'll tell you in a minute."

Wait, say what? In a minute? was going through my mind but at that time I could hear a still, small voice in my heart saying,

"Calm down, relax and don't say anything until you're asked to." I knew that had to be the holy spirit because I was not in the mood to calm down or relax at all. I was so scared I was literally shaking.

The next thing I knew, the 2 men that grabbed me were on their walkie-talkies, then as I actually started to calm down, I turned to my right and left and noticed not just the two men who grabbed me, but 6 other men standing around me. Then I looked at what they were wearing, and they all had on dark colors and vests on that said "US Marshal," with guns and other objects on them everywhere. I mean it looked like something out a movie or one of those cops shows I liked to watch.

After about 10 minutes of talking among themselves and whoever was on their radios, finally one of the men started asking questions. It was at that point I realized they had taken everything out of my pockets. I had on a jogging suit and only had my wallet, phone, and keys to Beacon in it, maybe some gum also.

Then I was asked to sit in a car while still handcuffed and surrounded, waiting. Then I was asked to stand up again, and the same guy asked,

"How tall are you"?

"5 foot, 10 inches," I said.

"Are you sure?" he responded.

"Yes, I'm sure," I said with an attitude.

By this time the fear was turning to anger or at least somewhat annoyance, but I kept hearing the still, small voice tells me,

" Remain calm, keep quiet, and don't say anything until you're told. Don't even speak with an attitude."

Just Believe, Don't Perform

Next thing I knew I was told to sit down again, so I did for what ended up being around 30 more minutes. As I looked at the clock in the officer's car, I realized I had been there for an hour from the time I remembered leaving Beacon to go on my walk downtown.

Finally, one of the other Marshals who hadn't said anything to me up to that point came over to me and speaks,

"Ok sir, I'm going to ask you to stand up, then turn around and we'll take the cuffs off. Then I'm going to tell you why we stopped you".

So, I then stood up and did what he said, the cuffs were taken off, and I turned around to face him as he began to speak.

TROY BARNES

"Mr. Barnes the reason we stopped you today is because you actually fit the description of a man we've been looking for since the late 2000s. A child rapist who committed the crime in Michigan and has been seen in other states such as Tennessee, Ohio and of course California, so he's been on the run."

Now I'll be honest, when they showed me a picture of the guy, I thought we looked nothing like except for maybe one picture where he's bald, but that certainly doesn't constitute me looking like him and a child rapist?! I then found out the reason they were holding me was to not only verify my identity, but they also went inside Beacon to verify who

I was as well and had even got in touch with Shannon to verify my ID as well.

When it was all over and I was free to go, the first person I saw calling my phone was Shannon. I was kind of nervous to talk to her since I had just started staying there and was wondering if she would be skeptical of me and maybe ask me to leave but she did the opposite.

"I knew that wasn't you they were talking about," she said. "I knew the guy they're looking for is not you, but I can't even imagine how you felt. Just horrible."

We actually laughed a little about the whole thing after she made sure I was ok. I knew there would be a lesson learned from all this, and God would use it to get the glory. And

it is now I know why as I begin to write my

second book. What's God saying through this

ordeal? **Just Believe, Don't Perform**

Just Believe, Don't Perform

Chapter Three:

Trusting God in The Midst of it All

When I was in this situation, I knew I was 100% innocent and had done nothing wrong, but there was still that 1 percent of doubt that tried to play in my mind, the feeling that "well maybe I did something I just forgot about" or maybe I was wrong, but I knew better and just shut that thought down.

In a lot of ways, it is the same way the enemy will play on our minds or emotions and say "Well maybe God's promises aren't true, maybe you are struggling because God is mad at you, because you've messed up big time now and you're going to be cursed. Maybe God doesn't love you after all and everything that preacher told you on Sunday was a lie."

Or maybe you're in a boring or dull marriage/relationship and the enemy is saying, "leave him or leave her, you'll have more fun being single anyway, right?!" (Be careful with that one, sometimes the grass isn't always greener on the other side. Sometimes that grass could be artificial turf).

I'm sure these things have come to mind when you're in a struggle or any case of hardship in life, but this is why it's important to not just go to church or perform just to try and show everyone you're a Christian, but actually to understand what the word of God says and know his promises.

When I was in the situation with the US Marshals, there wasn't any performance I could give to get me out of it. I knew I was innocent, but I still had to sit there and let everything run its course until I was free to go. The point is I still had to believe and trust myself, that was all I could do in that moment. Had I done anything else it could have turned out bad even though I knew I hadn't done anything wrong and would later be free to go.

Hebrews 11:6 says, "Anyone who wants to come to him must believe that God exists and that he rewards those who SINCERELY seek him."

Not just go to church, bible study or a Christian

group and "perform" but, know and believe

what his promises are for every area of life.

Chapter Four

Going Through the Motions

What I have found over the years is that most people know how to do church but don't know how to do "life". An example of this would be someone who goes to church every time the doors are open, pays their tithe, reads their bible every single night, attends every revival, prayer meeting, and does all kind of community work such as food banks, but in their heart, they don't walk in the ultimate commandment Jesus gave in John 13:34, which is *love*.

Just Believe, Don't Perform

Jesus says in this passage "So now I am giving you a new commandment: Love each other. Just as I have loved you, you should love each other. Your love for one another will prove to the world you are my disciples." Notice Jesus didn't say your "works" would prove we are his disciples, but his *love* is what proves we are his.

I realized works are only great and most effective when done in love. Otherwise, you're just performing and not really believing in the God, you claim you serve.

Another example of Jesus teaching on our belief versus performance is in the book of John, Chapter 6. Jesus was talking to a crowd of people that went looking for him in Capernaum after they had seen him do miracles and in verse 26, he told them "I'll tell you the truth, you want to be with me because I fed you, not because you understood the miraculous signs. But don't be so concerned about perishable things like food. Spend your energy seeking the eternal life that the Son of Man can give you. For God, the Father has given me the seal of approval."

Then in chapters 28 and 29 they replied "We want to perform God's works, too. What should we do?"

Then Jesus told them "This is the only work God wants from you: Believe in the one he has sent."

Just Believe, Don't Perform

That's all, just believe don't perform. Now by no way am I saying don't ever do good works. What I am saying is whatever you do make sure you do it with the right heart or intent. What I realized was while I was in situations where I couldn't do anything but seek him, or as Matthew 6:33 says "seek him FIRST," while I was seeking him the works I did would follow. Why? Because as I was spending time seeking him, he would place his desires in my heart and then I would do what truly pleases him, because I was doing it by faith and not because I felt I had to out of obligation.

It was at that point I began to love to serve, love to go to church, love to study the word of God, love to give whether it was my time or money, and love to serve the community I was in. I felt like I was in a real relationship with God, who is the heavenly father, and it was because of what Jesus had done for me.

I relate it to a marriage, like when you do things for your husband or wife because you love them, not just because you feel obligated. What wife wants her husband to be there just out of obligation and not because he really loves her and enjoys her company, can't wait to come home to her, or misses her deeply when he's not with her.

Just Believe, Don't Perform

This is what it truly means to be "saved." Not just so you go to the kingdom of heaven when you leave this earth but also experience great things while still on Earth. To experience the true blessings of God. It's all part of what I talked about in my last book. All part of his Amazing Grace, his unmerited, undeserved favor.

Most of the time earlier in my life I always felt like I had to do all the normal "church" stuff, or I was disappointing God. Otherwise, he wouldn't bless me or make me a blessing to others, which at times left me pretty unfulfilled. While I was always grateful for how I grew up, in a two-parent home with a stable family, many friends who I knew from school or work, and seeming to flourish on every job I had, there was always something missing. I knew there was more to my life, and I always felt a calling to do more for God, I just was never sure what it would be.

I realized it took a few hardships in order to move me into positions to truly receive from him and to truly believe him and his word. It's one thing to hear or read God's word especially while going to church on Sunday but it's a whole other thing when you're in a position where you have to apply it.

Being homeless, in debt, having no money or being in a place with not a lot of resources will do that do you. Everyone has a testimony or story of their own but it's how you stand in the middle of the situation that will determine your outcome.

Chapter Five:

No Wavering

When I moved to California in 2017 and was let go from the very job that brought me here, I had to stand on God's word and see him with my whole heart, not just halfway. I had to make God's word my own. As the scripture says, "Death and Life are in the power of the tongue" - Proverbs 18:21. The word of God also says "You are snared by the words of your mouth" - Proverbs 6:2, but also that "Christ is the high priest over our confessions" - Hebrews 4:14 meaning he's like an advocate over our spoken words as long as it's his word we're speaking.

Many times, what we accuse the enemy of is not really him at all. It's really the fruit of negative confessions. Your words will either bring life or death to a situation. The tense in which you declare a thing is crucial, because if you are always using the future tense when making declarations then it keeps it from manifesting today. Our confessions need to be present tense and not so much future tense if we want to see the manifestation of it today.

For example, saying I will be healed vs "by the stripes of Jesus I am healed" (Isaiah 53:5). A perfect example of this is found in

Romans 4:17 where it says to "call those things that be not as though they were". Meaning to call those things to pass as if they have already happened.

Hebrews 11:1 says, "NOW faith is the substance of things hoped for and the evidence of things not seen."

And I believe the ultimate example is I Thessalonians 5: 16:18. "Rejoice always, pray without ceasing, and in everything give thanks; for this is the will of God in Christ Jesus for you."

I'm a big believer in the attitude of gratitude or that your attitude is your altitude. You may not always be responsible for the situation you find yourself in; but you are responsible for how you come through or out of

it.

Chapter Six:

Drama

One morning while I was in the middle of my 2 ½ month stay at the Mission homeless shelter in Long Beach I did what I did every day there. Got up at 6am, which is standard as that's when they woke everyone up, went downstairs to get my suitcase of clothes to figure out what I was going to throw on for the day (showers are done at night before bedtime) got my little bag of toiletries and walked over to the one of 5 sinks in the large downstairs community bathroom to brush my teeth.

While all of this is normal there, on this particular morning; I was about to find myself in a situation I hadn't been in for a very long time, since maybe high school. There was an open sink as the other sinks were taken by residents doing the same thing I was trying to do, put on deodorant, brush their teeth, etc. when suddenly one of the guys there just pushed me out of the way as I was brushing my teeth.

I didn't even notice him coming but needless to say at that point I absolutely lost it! I pushed him right back just as hard as he pushed me. I was pissed off at that point and said,

"WHO THE HELL DO YOU THINK YOU ARE TO PUT YOUR HANDS ON ME?"

I think I said, something like that. I obviously was not having it. I already was in one of those moods that morning just trying to make it through the early part of the day. It was mentally tough being in a shelter as I was still not understanding why I had to be there in the first place, not understanding my assignment with God yet.

Next thing I knew we both fell to the ground and were wrestling around on the floor which carried us all the way to the shower just behind us. As I was trying to swing on him, two of the workers there pulled us off of each other. As we got up, I realized we had a crowd of people around us. Now here is the interesting part, it is standard that if there's any fighting you're automatically kicked out or asked to leave. With me though, no one said a single word to the guy who started it, I found out later, he was gone that day.

Now the guy that did it I had seen since I'd been at the shelter, and he was one of the ones that did not look mentally stable. I saw him at times wandering around having an attitude and talking to himself, so I was not surprised he was gone but it was nothing but God's grace that kept me from being asked to leave. I mean, where was I going to go? I had a little money but not enough to do anything with, I did not know anyone so I would have been on the street, but God's grace kept me until it was time to go. He had me covered all along and all I could do was just believe. I certainly didn't perform. I would have failed that performance anyway.

Just Believe, Don't Perform

Chapter Seven:

My Family Life

The most humbling experience of my life was being homeless and staying at the homeless shelter in Long Beach after being let go from the job that brought me to California. Growing up in Ohio all I knew was being in a Christian home with two parents, my father and mother, along with my brother Lee.

Going to school as a kid (and a mostly shy one at that) and always growing up in nice neighborhoods, having nice clean clothes, shoes and living more middle class than anything was just the norm I thought. My parents always made sure we had what we needed and even at times a little more and were completely satisfied with that, but we were always taught to be grateful for what we had. My parents did an excellent job of showing me and my brother Lee about not just talking about it but being about it when it came to living within our means and they were great examples for me. They taught me about being grateful not just by saying but by doing.

Watching them made me appreciate life and try not to take things for granted. We also had balance as a family. My dad was the strict one and he certainly did not take any mess.

TROY BARNES

Coming from the south and a military background also he would let us know when we were out of line quick. A couple times he did so with a belt or butt whooping as they used to call it. Nowadays you cannot do that anymore as it's called "child abuse." In my family and many others back in the day it was called "discipline" which obviously is missing in today's world which is why I believe there are so many more shootings, killings and murders along with other crimes. People are more reckless now than ever which is all way too sad.

My dad only had to whoop my behind twice that I remember and that was even too many, but what it did was make me have respect not only for him but others as well. Still my dad was always providing for the family buying groceries or allowing us to get what we needed for the start of school every year, and of course holidays and Christmas. Even treating us to dinner on the weekends. I remember as a kid at times during the summer he would take us out for ice cream.

My mom on the other hand brought the faith to our family, taking me and my brother Lee to church when we were little. At a very early age, as far back as I can remember my mom was the one who led the charge of making sure we had Christian values instilled in our lives because she was the one always doing it herself.

It caused me to give my life to Jesus and become "saved" around the age of 12, even getting baptized at the church we were going to. I would attend Sunday school at times and Vacation Bible School for a week during the summer as I was always wanting to learn more about God. I cannot even imagine a life without the Lord thanks to my mom and what she did. Little did I know back then how much I would need Him later in life.

My mom would also take us shopping, to the movies and was always wanting to talk. My dad worked a lot even on weekends at times, so we would spend more time with mom when she wasn't working or taking care of her sister, my aunt Helen who was born with a developmental disability. This meant Helen was like a child or had the mind of one even though she grew older.

She came to live with us when I was a teenager after my grandfather passed and my grandmother had a heart attack and could no longer live on her own or take care of my aunt. My mom had fulfilled a promise she made to my grandparents that she would never let anyone, or anything take my aunt Helen or have her left in a home care facility somewhere. That was a whole other faith walk watching my mom take care of her like she was her only daughter.

My aunt Helen could feed herself, put on her own clothes, bathe herself and all but you just had to tell her to do it. Sometimes she would tell you she was going to do it just like a child would, which made us laugh. Sometimes she would laugh too as if to say, "I know what I'm doing." My aunt lived till her mid 60's before passing away which was a testimony in and of itself.

My mom would also take us over to our Grandparent's house or to visit other relatives and friends of hers as well. With all that being said, don't get it twisted my mom could dish out her own discipline on us too. I remember one time getting in trouble over at my Grandparents and her going outside and getting a switch off a tree to whoop me with for talking back. Glad I got through those days.

My brother Lee and I had a typical brother to brother relationship, usually playing video games, watch football, basketball or WWF wrestling as kids, even acting out what we saw on TV with one of us being Hulk Hogan and the other being Macho Man Randy Savage or the Ultimate Warrior. As we got older and in high school, we did what everyone else did, made a lot of friends, and went to neighborhood or city parks to play sports. We also went to after school functions such as dances, various sporting events, high school prom etc.

While no family is perfect, and all of them have their issues, everything I experienced growing up was what I thought of as normal, not giving much thought to it being anything else. In my teen years, I found out I had another brother named Robert. I initially thought he was my cousin when we were kids because I would see him at family functions like our family reunions or family outings my grandparents would have. It wasn't until I was around 13 or 14 (I think) that I and Lee were told he was our brother from a previous relationship my dad had before marrying my mom.

Just Believe, Don't Perform

I was shocked at first and obviously, there was a lot going on in the family however I didn't really think about it after that. We all have a past, and I looked at it as "if he's my dad's son then he's my brother just like my brother Lee and we're all still a family and I love him no less."

There was always so much fun when we; along with my other cousins such as Eric, Randy, and Wendell Jr (Randy and Wendell Jr lived in Mississippi so we didn't get to see them often,) would get together. There was always so much clowning around and laughing till my stomach would hurt.

Chapter Eight:

Something Changed

As I got older, graduated high school, started working, and eventually went to college at a community college in downtown Columbus. Then I eventually moved out of my parent's house and got my first apartment, and I started being invited to go out with friends a lot, sometimes all weekend long. It was at that moment I realized I was going out all the time and not attending church as I grew up doing.

Just Believe, Don't Perform

I began to start feeling bad about it as if something was missing in my life, so I started attending a church nearby, a rather large one at that. The church I grew up in was way across town and after a night of partying on Saturday it was difficult to get up on Sunday and drive all the way to the other side of town. At the time I just looked at it as "ok I went to church so I did my good deed for the week," in a very religious way, however, the more I kept going the more I would hear things said in the sermons that hit me.

Sometimes these things hit me right in the heart and even though I would function as though nothing happened outside, on the inside I knew God was speaking to me about certain things in my life, mostly about getting closer to him. Then I started reading the bible and I began to study and tie scriptures into what the preacher was saying. I started to learn what various scriptures mean and how to apply them to my life.

Now it didn't happen overnight as nothing does and I still made a lot of mistakes but what God was doing was building a foundation for his word in me. I then began to get involved in serving and volunteering. I started in the youth ministry of the church and took on several jobs.

Just Believe, Don't Perform

One job I had was driving one of the church vans to downtown Columbus and picking up some youth from the inner-city and taking them to our youth Services on Sunday nights. That was interesting because I made a connection with a couple of the youths I picked up and started befriending, talking, and praying with them.

After about six months of that along with serving in various other parts of the ministry, I was asked by one of the leaders to replace him as a teacher of a class geared towards the youth. I never looked at myself as a teacher and initially did not want any part of public speaking, standing in front of anyone having to talk scared me to death but then I began to feel the desire to do it. Plus, with the materials we were given to use in the classes I said to myself "I know this stuff" so I decided I would do it.

It was challenging for sure but what helped me a lot was picturing in my mind how others I admired would get up and speak to people and then I would just copy them. That helped me get comfortable until I could make the class my own while still teaching the material we were given. I still do that to this day when speaking in front of people, all while allowing God to use me as well.

Just Believe, Don't Perform

One thing that did happen while serving in the youth ministry was that it began to start the change, or at least planted the idea that there was more to my relationship with God than I knew at that time. One weeknight our youth pastor at the time who we all called Brother Joey had scheduled a meeting with the youth leaders of the ministry. This was typical as we usually met once a month.

Towards the end of the meeting, he asked all the leaders to line up in the front of the room we were in as he was going to pray for us. He ended up going to each individual leader one by one praying and in some cases doing what they call "laying hands" on them. I never really liked and was comfortable with this type of ministry not because I don't believe it may not work for some people that need to receive the word from God through a Pastor or leader but I am not comfortable with it for me!

I always used to wonder "Is all this really necessary to receive blessings from God?" I mean there are many in the bible who received from Jesus just by what he said. I read in the book of Matthew Chapter 8 about a centurion who had a servant that was suffering. He was paralyzed and when Jesus was going to heal him the guy said to Jesus, "Speak the word and my servant will be healed." He was healed in that same moment.

Just Believe, Don't Perform

In any case I stood there and waited for him to get to me, feeling more nervous and anxious than anything else. He finally gets to me and as I bow my head, close my eyes to wait to hear what he says he then says something to the effect of this

"Troy, you are a people person. Your gift is with people and for people. God is going to use you in a mighty way to affect people because of your heart. Let him use you, don't fight it, just let him use you and you will see his goodness overflow in your life says, God."

After that, he went on to the next person. *That's it?* I thought as I then went to sit down, kind of surprised. I was expecting something more animated like I was seeing with others. With me though he was just as calm and cool as can be. I wasn't even sure what to think since at the time I was still very shy and timid most of the time. I usually wanted to hurry and get away from people, so I do not have to say much. But isn't it just like God to take your weakness and use it for his purpose and glory!

Just Believe, Don't Perform

Chapter Nine

Building A Relationship With Christ

I kept thinking about the encounter I had. Over the course of the next several weeks I started to feel better about it, although I still had no idea how I could be used. One thing I did know at that time, and still know to this day is I didn't just want to do "church as usual" or get up on stage and preach like a performer.

Not that I'm against what God has called anyone else to do, I am by no means judge or jury and I don't want to be a judge as to what's right and what's not. God uses everyone in every way. I spent about 5 years at this church and ministry serving before eventually moving to another part of town.

When moving to other parts of town I would always try to find a church within 15 to 20 minutes from where I lived to go to. I was always faithful to go every Sunday no matter what I did the night before (or several nights before in some cases).

I would go to church, read my bible, give my tithe and offering, not all the time but I did when I felt I could, serve in some capacity or area, and in all of that I thought I was being faithful. To be real and honest most of the time

I went to church I felt as if I was made to feel as though I had to do all those things to get in good with God.

I felt like because there was so much emphasis on the "works" part of Christianity I lost or hid who I really was, a flawed person who can make mistakes at any time and who needs God's grace and love just like anyone. Just like we all do.

This is why I believe God allowed me to go through the last several years, and even being unemployed a couple of times so I could study, be educated and experience the true meaning of his "Amazing Grace" which is the gospel of Jesus Christ. It's not just a song we can sing in church on Sundays, it's a way of life, "THE" way of life God wants us to live.

A year before moving to California I started attending a church near where I lived on the west side of Columbus whereas I was starting to study about God's grace, I was able to start to see it working. My friend Lorna had started inviting me to this church and I really enjoyed going mainly because of the people. I met a lot of genuinely good people who just wanted to serve and worship God.

As I met and got to know a few of the men who were leading, one of them invited me to a weekly men's bible study that went on every Thursday night. There was a lot of roundtable discussion about the scriptures we were going over and the leader who we called "Coach Williams" was an older guy that was ran the study. We all had opportunities to speak and for some reason he really liked and felt everything I said and added in our discussions to the point where after a couple of months of going he started asking me to lead the studies, even calling me and asking to fill in when he couldn't be there.

What I thought I would be afraid to do I ended up really enjoying, and the responses to my teaching were pretty positive. That eventually led to an opportunity to speak at a big men's fellowship where I got to speak to about 60 men on a Friday night for an hour or so. I look back on these experiences as God continuing to build that foundation and preparing me for what was to come once, I moved to California. Although I do still miss the people at the church to this day.

What God showed me and revealed to me while I was homeless after losing my job in Long Beach was that all of those "works" don't equal a sustaining relationship with him. While all those things are good to do while in a relationship with him, they mean absolutely nothing if you are not doing it in love and walking by faith. Otherwise, you are just being religious.

Another word that comes to mind is *robotic.* What does that mean? Just doing things on schedule or because you are "supposed to," or because that's what you were told, or because "everyone else is doing it". Truth is that does not take any faith.

That is living under the Law of Moses and not under Grace and Truth which is what God wants us to live by. Don't believe me, that's what the scripture says in John 1:17 "For the law was given through Moses, but God's grace (unmerited favor or unfailing love) and truth came through Jesus Christ." So yes, I accepted

Just Believe, Don't Perform

Christ as a kid and believed in him, but I was not walking with him the way I needed to, by faith, because I was doing what I thought I knew to do.

Just do all the "works" and God will bless you, everything will be easy, so I thought. Then when things would go wrong in my life, I thought it was always because I failed God, meaning failed to do the works. Maybe it was because I missed church on a Sunday, I didn't give my offering, didn't pray hard enough, or maybe long enough for God to be pleased with me, or I didn't read my bible because I was too busy watching sports or whatever. All the while I knew in my heart there was more, more I felt inspired to do for God, but I just didn't know what, and in part was afraid to find out what it would be.

I wasn't truly walking with him in what I call "Relationship Based Prayer." I had gained a lot of knowledge about the word of God, but I needed to get to know him. To know him truly for myself.

So now, back to being at the homeless shelter in 2017, God was showing me that he had allowed me to be in the position so he could move me into something greater. He wanted to pull out the gifts and talents he needed in me in order to use me, so I could truly and fully surrender all to him, but also for the purpose of helping other people like Shannon and my

Beacon for Him family. I would not have been equipped to serve there or anywhere like I was doing without first letting go and believing in God. God doesn't do anything without a purpose, unlike men or women who can do anything, and it means nothing.

Chapter Ten:

NO Failure in God

Now I have to be totally honest and transparent with you, there were times I was mad, mad at God, mad at myself for feeling like I failed in getting into this position, being homeless, and not understanding what was going on. Fear tried to take over but I don't like being afraid or worrying at all so I would always reject that. 2 Timothy 1:7 says, "God didn't give us the spirit of fear but that he gave us power, love, and a sound mind or self-control."

It could have been easy for me to slip into depression or even worse. See for someone like me who has mostly been more an introvert and always been typically shy, not wanting to talk or even at times not be around people because either I get too anxious around people or not knowing how to deal with people who get on my nerves at times, to be found in the situation of being homeless or displaced can be damaging to one's mind. I can honestly say the way I was cost me the opportunity at several relationships I could have had in dating women because of feeling past hurts or even nearly dating someone I could have but the thought of them saying no if I asked felt humiliating to me and it was all fear based.

Fear is paralyzing and not how God wants us to live. I realized while homeless that one, I had to give everything in my past up, including myself and how I used to be to Him. And two, he was having me learn how to truly walk by faith and not rely on my performance with him (to see if I checked all the spiritual boxes) while at the same time build a REAL relationship with him where I can pray and talk to him anytime, about anything, all the time.

Get this, I can even talk to him about how I feel about certain situations, when I mess up, do right or wrong, even the littlest of things, talk to him just like you would a best friend or partner. I can rest in the fact that he loves me just like he loves Jesus.

One of the difficult times in the process came just a few weeks into my stay at the shelter and volunteering at Beacon for Him ministries. I had just gotten to the church to start working and my cell phone was about to die, and I needed a place to charge it, so I left it along with my charger in what I thought was a safe place.

I was serving in the kitchen at the time and left it plugged in at an outlet just behind me while I served. While there I ended up leaving the kitchen several times just going around helping and as we were finishing up for the day, I forgot that I had left my phone in the kitchen where I started. I go back to get it and guess what?! Charger is there but no phone. I almost lost it right there, but I remained calm, asked everyone I could if they had seen it, looked everywhere I could and absolutely nothing. It was GONE!

How upsetting that I'm now without a job, transportation, without a home and now no phone along with the fact I could not remember anyone's phone number to contact them. Fortunately, I remembered I had insurance on the phone and just needed to get to a carrier to order a replacement. Shannon graciously took me to one that day so I could file a claim and I was able to order a new one, but they said it would take 10 to 14 days to arrive.

"say what?!?!.... I cannot wait that long!" Isn't there something you can do? Well, you can buy a new phone... I had to stop them there since at the time I did not have the money. Unreal, as here I am now trying to look for a job, trying to keep in contact with especially my mom among other people so they don't think I'm dead but also in case someone calls with a job opportunity as I had just submitted my now revised and all new resume out to recruiters and various job websites.

TROY BARNES

So long story short I went and waited a full two weeks for the new phone to arrive and it look every day of it. Even when I would use the landline at Beacon or Shannon's phone to call the insurance department every other day the answer was still "in 10 to 14 days." On the last possible day, the new phone finally showed up but not before I learned a valuable lesson in it all.

While I was without a phone and couldn't talk to hardly anyone it also meant I couldn't use it to check social media or be on the internet. It was a pretty hurtful thing to open up Facebook and Instagram only to see all of your connected friends and family posting about the good times they were having.

Whether it was getting together for dinners, going to football games or tailgating before, celebrating birthday parties or just a night out on the town, it was not fun at all seeing all of that, and being in the situation I was in, staying where I was staying in a homeless shelter confined with a curfew of going to bed every night at 8pm. I remember thinking to myself many times early on that "I did not come to California for all of this."

What it did do however was force me to seek God's word and promises and meditate on them. To start using them daily with hardly any distractions. Waking up in the morning and confessing God's word, talking to him, thanking him, reading daily devotionals, whatever it took to fill my mind and keep me at peace. To be honest, by the time my new phone arrived I had developed not only true peace but a real habit of real prayers and daily confessions that I still use to this day.

One of the main ones is confession from the scripture John 17:23, that God loves me just as he loves his son Jesus. Also 1 John 4:17 says, "as he (Christ) is so are we in this world."

When you know someone loves you and you trust that they do you can be more vulnerable with them because you trust they aren't out to hurt you. I have always had issues trusting other people which was my downfall in some cases with relationships. Sometimes it is just feeling the need to have to perform instead of just being myself.

Why would I do that you ask? For fear, someone may not like or appreciate me. Well same way with God, why would I try to perform to get the blessings of God? For fear, if I don't, I wouldn't be blessed by Him. I learned in scripture that it says "he has blessed us with all spiritual blessings in Christ" in Ephesians 1:3 so I don't have to do all of the "works" to get blessed, I already am blessed because of what Christ did for me.

Now God is a gentleman he will not ever force things on you, everyone has free will but when or if you do surrender to his will for your life, it will require faith for you to believe in what He has for you. Even if you would say you're not strong or you're weak, with what he's calling you to do remember how the scripture says in 2 Corinthians 12:9 "His strength is made perfect in your weakness."

Could I pray, yes, could I talk, of course, but could I pray and really talk to God? Could I really be used by God? Who would care what I have to say? "I don't have any talent" I would say to myself. I wasn't good enough to play sports, can't sing or rap, not an actor, never considered myself highly intelligent or with any huge gifts that would warrant really being used by God. So why would he?

All these were things I let play in my mind and I thought about while being homeless. But once I stopped looking at myself and focused on others who were homeless, displaced and in need around me, I realized I had a gift that was greater than any other. I had God by way of what Christ did on the cross and received him as my savior and the people around me at that time needed him. I had the knowledge of what I learned about God's grace, which is his unmerited, undeserved favor, the last several years of studying scriptures and getting the revelation for myself of what God's love is and how it is the holy spirit working through us that shows people about him.

It is about our loving walk with him that provides the faith people need to live each day. And it is his love that comforts and encourages us when we mess up and fall short, consoles us when we experience any type of loss, and empowers us to do great things for him and people. Learning these things enabled me and my relationship with him so I can walk by faith and not by sight as he says. It was literal on the job training.

Just Believe, Don't Perform

Chapter Eleven:

Favor with God and Man

I n my last book "Amazing Grace – My Journey into God's Unmerited Favor" I talked about my friend Rebecca who then managed, and now is part owner of a restaurant in Long Beach, the one who gave me my first car. The miracle in all that was it was the day before I started my first job after being let go from the previous one. I still remember that day like it was yesterday as I remember how I did not even see it coming.

Just Believe, Don't Perform

She gave me an old car, a 2004 Volkswagen, but I was so happy and appreciative of it I treated it like a new car. I had it fixed up a little both inside and out, took it to the car wash just about every weekend and drove it almost everywhere I went. I mean who does that, just give away cars to people??

People who have giving hearts and people who are sent and used by God whether they realize it or not, that's who, and It's definitely who my friend is as she would give her last dime to someone in need. I am thankful to be surrounded by people like this all the time. Even when the car needed repairs, I would get it fixed as soon as I could. Because it was an old car with a ton of miles the amount of work it needed began to add up, but I fixed what I could, just believing God would provide. I mean he got me the car so why wouldn't I think he would provide for it?

He's proven to be a God of his word; he just requires us to have faith. Roman 1:17 and Galatians 3:11 says "the just or righteous shall live by faith" so I always knew I'd be ok no matter what. One day while talking to another friend of mine named Bas, he asked me if I knew anyone looking to buy a car? At the time I did as one of my roommates was in the market for one. Bas took out his phone and showed me photos of the car he was trying to sell.

Just Believe, Don't Perform

It was a beautiful white BMW X3 SUV. I told him my roommate was looking at BMW's and would probably want to take a look at it but when I mentioned it to him later that evening it wasn't the model he was wanting and had already set his sights on another model which he then got a couple of weeks later. I told Bas I would ask around to help him out but while I was doing this more problems started to arise with my own car.

One early Saturday morning while looking online I found a small auto center about 15 minutes from where I lived and so I took it in, hoping for the best but kind of nervous it would be more than I could afford at that time. He gave me a list of things wrong with it after running all of the diagnostics and sure enough, it was more than I could afford. He did tell me that if I could get 2 of the 5 things it needed fixed it would help it run a little longer, so I was able to take care of those that day. Because he would need to keep the car for the day, he even gave me a loaner car to drive for free until he finished with my car (more of God's favor working for me). I picked my car back up around the shop's closing time and drove around for another month with no real visible problems.

As I'm talking to my friend Bas about the issues, I was starting to have with my car he says to me,

Just Believe, Don't Perform

"Well, you know I told you I'm selling my car why don't I just sell you mine?

"But it's a BMW" I said, "I can't afford that and don't even need that."

As I pulled out my phone to look at the photos of the car that he sent me to show my roommate, at that moment I heard this still small voice in my heart say, "take the car." At nearly the exact same time my friend says to me, I'll work with you on a payment plan, but I really would like to sell it. I decline again saying, oh no I do not need all that. I do not need a BMW that is too much. We laugh about it and move on from the conversation. About a week later the engine light on my car comes on. GREAT... I thought, now this.

As I start praying immediately because I started getting nervous, especially with what I knew still needed to be fixed with it, I then keep hearing in my heart, "take the BMW, tell your friend you'll take it." I was being so stubborn because in my mind I kept thinking I cannot afford that. I even asked the company I worked for if they rent cars as a backup even though I was hired in as a contractor and not a full-time employee, but I was still working full-time hours.

All the while I just kept feeling like I needed to take my friend's car. After another week of being stubborn, I saw my friend and finally put my pride away and asked him about his car. I asked Bas if I could stop by and take it for a drive.

"Absolutely," he said. "Come over this Thursday." So, I did.

Once we got in the car and I started driving it felt really good. I mean it's a BMW. It had been so long since I had driven a really nice car, I almost forgot what it felt like. He was kind of laughing at me as I was being kind of timid behind the wheel. "

Are you ok"? He asked laughing while we were talking, "you can drive faster" he said.

"I'm just getting the feel of it, just trying to get comfortable," I said.

It was so very nice. I drove it for about 20 minutes while all I kept hearing in my heart was, "TAKE THE CAR. TELL HIM YOU'LL TAKE THE CAR RIGHT NOW!" When we pulled back up to his house, I told him

"Ok I will take the car, we'll have to work out a payment plan, but I will take it." We spent the next week settling on an agreement and it's a good thing we did because my car was starting to get worse. It was running kind of rough and feeling as though it was on its last leg.

On a Sunday morning I had gotten up and went to church in my neighborhood then went to Long Beach to serve at Beacon for Him ministries. My pastor (Pastor Clark) who I mentioned in my last book, was holding church service for the homeless there every Sunday.

Even though it was in a different and much smaller building we still wanted to provide a church for those who couldn't make it to a church home anywhere else, so every Sunday we served.

Thanks again to Shannon James, the president and founder of the ministry for keeping it going.

As I hit the 405 freeway, leaving Long Beach I looked down at my dashboard and noticed that the temperature gauge was moving more and more to the right, giving an indication my engine is running hot. I had about

30 miles to get home so I got there as fast as I could.

The good thing about this was I had worked it out with my friend Bas that I could get the BMW this very week. The other good thing was that it was Christmas break and the company I work for closes for the Christmas and New Year's holiday so there was really no where I had to go this week except for when I was invited to spend Christmas with my friend Dawn and her family, but I wasn't worried about getting to her house. I knew I could just Uber if nothing else.

At this time, I had also started looking into selling my car. Because it was so old and needed a lot of work it basically had no value so all I could get for it was $250. I called several places and found a place that would take a look at it, but I had to take it to them. It was only 10 minutes away, so I asked one of my roommates who was home at the time to go with me, but drive behind me just in case something happened, and I didn't make it. Well guess what!?

Something did happen, it started overheating and the engine started smoking really badly, to the point I almost couldn't see so I had to pull over in a parking lot while I called my insurance for a tow. Then when I called the place that was going to look at my car, I actually got them to come to me, but they wouldn't take it because of the condition it was in, so I just had my insurance tow it back home. Later that week Bas brought me the BMW and a week later I was able to sell my now old car to a junkyard for $200 dollars, probably more than it was even worth at that point.

Once again by God's grace, I now had what felt like a new car that was in great condition. He even had maintenance done and new tires put on it for me before dropping it off. As it has been with me so far, everything was working out and the timing could not have worked out better. Even in my stubbornness, doubt, and any mistakes I made, it was just another example of just believing and not performing. Another example of how God took care of me again as he promised.

Chapter Twelve:

The Righteousness of God

I want to now talk about what it means to be the righteousness of God. This is important because it deals with our identity as a Christian, our relationship with God, and how we interact or relate to him. First off 2 Corinthians 5:17 says this, "Therefore if any man be in Christ, he is a new creature, old things are pass away behold all things are become new". When you make Jesus' lord of your life you are made to be a new creation in God's eyes.

Just Believe, Don't Perform

The old man or I should say the old spirit of a man is now gone and a new spirit man takes over. That old man had a sinful nature but once you receive Christ as lord you take on a new nature in a process that's similar to what Jesus did on the cross. *Let me insert this here also... the very thing the world celebrates once a year as Easter, we can celebrate every day of our lives because of who we are in Christ and because we have received him as lord. That also means we can receive the benefits of Christ. More on this later.*

Because you are a new creation and have been made the righteousness of God you are now no longer a sinner but now, because of what Jesus did on the cross you are saved by HIS grace…. Let me say this again… you are now saved by HIS grace and not your own. His performance and not your own. His finished work on the cross and not any of your works down on earth. Do you understand? Are you getting it?

You are now righteous because of your belief and receiving of Christ and no longer a sinner or carry the sinful nature. Now that also doesn't mean you will never sin again, we all do, but what sin actually means is to "miss the mark". We all miss the mark from time to time, some people may say all the time (I know I do), but because you have received Christ and his spirit now lives on the inside of you, you no longer have to live under the condemnation of sin or missing the mark.

When you make a mistake just repent and turn away from it or just STOP! What this also means is that sin has no authority over you. Romans 6:14 "For sin will have no dominion over you: for you are not under the law, but under GRACE" (meaning the law of Moses i.e., the 10 commandments and all of the other 613 laws in the Old Testament).

When you make a mistake or miss the mark you can't get down on yourself and say, "oh well I'm just an old sinner saved by grace". That's foolish, you can't be a sinner and saved by grace at the same time. You're either one or the other and if you have received Christ then you are no longer a sinner, you are now *saved by grace*!

Don't believe me, study these scriptures for yourself. This is extremely important in your walk and relationship with God and will save you a ton of condemnation and disappointment. God is love and his plan, according to 3 John 2 is to "prosper and you be in health even as your soul prospers".

Your soul is your mind, your will and your emotions and the word of God tells us how to control our mind. Romans 12:2 says to "not be conformed to this world but to be transformed by the renewal of your mind, that by testing you may discern what is the acceptable and perfect will of God".

Now it's also important not to take what I'm saying and think you can just live any kind of way you want or become boastful and full of pride. That's called "Self-righteousness" and that is certainly not what I'm saying. As a matter of fact, Romans 12:3 says, "For I say, by the grace given to me, to every man that is among you, not to think of himself more highly than he ought to think; but think soberly, according as God has dealt to every man the measure of faith".

Bottom line is it's important to stay humble knowing it is through Christ we have this relationship and no one else. We're not in Christ because we're all that, we are who we are in Christ because *he's all that*!

One of things that just about blew me away when studying our relationship with God in regard to sin was a few other scriptures. Romans 4:8 says, "Blessed is the man whose sin whom the lord will not impute (count against) him." Jesus and his blood that was shed for us has completely washed away our sins as part of being in relationship with him. Not just past sins, not just present sins, but future sins as well.

Just Believe, Don't Perform

Jesus had to do what he did for all sins of humanity so we could be in right standing with God our father and this is why we call him savior. Now, God has promised us when we mess up or miss the mark, we can come to him as a son or daughter would their father and he will do what Hebrews 8:12-13 says, "And I will forgive their wickedness and I will never remember their sins again". And "when God speaks of a "new" covenant, it means he has made the first one obsolete. It is now out of date and will disappear." The first covenant spoken here is the law of Moses from the Old Testament but the new one is the covenant of Grace which comes by only one name, Jesus.

2 Corinthians 5:21 says "God made him who had no sin to be sin for us, so that in him we could become the righteousness of God." The him who God made or is referring to is Jesus, and the word righteousness means "to be in right standing" so putting it all together we're in right standing with God right now not based on works but based on faith.

Galatians 3:11 says "For in it the righteousness of God is reveled from faith to faith, as it is written the righteous or just shall live by faith." Hebrews 11:6 says without this faith it is impossible to please him. What does all of this mean you ask?

Just Believe, Don't Perform

It means you have a right to all God's promises for your life no matter what situation you find yourself in. Mine was homelessness and lacking things, yours could be health related, finances, family, relationship, a bad marriage, business, politics and even something as severe as cancer or Covid-19. God has answers for *all of it*.

All he wants is for us to do as Matthew 6:33 says "Seek ye First the Kingdom of God and HIS righteousness and all things will be added to you." He wants us to make him a priority and seek him first.

Chapter Thirteen:

Seek God First

One situation that I've had to continually seek God on was with my job. When I was started on my current job for a car company in April 2018 it was done as a contractor through a 3rd party company. While I was beyond grateful for being blessed with the job, especially in my field of IT Asset Management, because I was a contractor it did not come with the full benefits typical jobs come with.

Just Believe, Don't Perform

If you're fortunate enough to be hired on as an actual employee, you not only get full benefits, but employees are eligible for bonuses and get this; a new car to drive as part of their car allowance program. I certainly didn't need all of this at the time, but my attitude was just one of gratitude that I got in the door and was able to start making a living and more importantly building a foundation for being here in California. Little did I know there was so much more God had in store, but like always I had to wait on his timing.

One day in July 2021 while meeting a few people for lunch, my boss and I got to the lunch spot at the same time so as we were walking from the parking garage to the restaurant, he told me

"Oh, by the way, your position as a contractor is being terminated, so they'll be letting you go."

Now my boss is a practical joker, so I didn't even take him seriously at first. My response was "ok yeah right LOL."

"No, I'm serious they're letting you go" he said.

"Ok whatever LOL again" I said.

Then he goes "I'm really serious…. Didn't you hear what you did?"

Now for some reason I started to get concerned as he was not smiling like usual when he says things.

"No what did I do?" I said. He then pulled out his phone and said, "Well here I'll show you."

Now I really did start to get incredibly nervous then he said,

"They're letting you go because congratulations, you're now an employee."

I almost didn't know whether to be happy or smack him but was very grateful that after over 3 years of being a contractor for the company I was now going to be an official employee. This means full benefits including bonuses and even more, the car allowance. Now I get a new car of my choice to drive as an employee benefit. How cool is that!? It turns out I was now going to need it.

It's Sunday toward the end of July and I had just gotten the good news about being hired as an official employee at the car company I worked for. I was on my way to Pastor Clark's church in Long Beach, a church he was just starting as we were no longer holding any services at Beacon for Him. I was driving down the 405 freeway and about 10 minutes from the exit at Long Beach Blvd, when I all of a sudden noticed something that looked like a long piece of metal, almost like a metal pipe, come flying off a pickup truck that was in front of me and start rolling towards me as I'm driving.

It was coming so fast I didn't have any time to react or try to switch lanes to move away from it for fear that I would swerve and hit someone else on either side of me, so I ran over it. It made a loud "BANG" sound and all I could do at that point was pray it didn't do any damage. I made it to church with no issues and I especially wanted to be there this day as it was Pastor's birthday, so we were there to celebrate.

We finished our services and celebration for his birthday, and I left to head back to Orange County. My house and neighborhood are about a 40-minute drive away on a good day of traffic. As I get on the 405-freeway driving home I remembered what happened, running over the metal piece before church but still no evidence that anything was wrong. Until about 5 minutes into the drive when I heard a loud beep, only to look down at the dashboard and see the following message, "Drive Train Malfunction"

"Oh no" I said to myself, then before I could do anything else I hear another loud beep, looked down at the dashboard again and saw the message "Low Oil" followed by another message, "Oil dangerously low, pull the vehicle over to avoid any damage to the engine"

Just Believe, Don't Perform

You must be kidding me was all I could think as I found the nearest exit, pulled off, and stopped at a gas station right off the exit. I knew I was not going to make it all the way home, so I called my insurance to ask for a tow truck to pick up the car. When the tow truck driver arrived, I asked him to take the car to a shop in Anaheim that I was referred to back when I got the car. I rode with the driver to make sure it got to the shop, and I could leave the key.

As were on the way there we started having small talk which then turned into a conversation about faith. The driver asked where I was from, and I started to go into my story, being from Ohio and moving out to

California. With each answer I gave him he had more questions, and this then led to me sharing my testimony with him (this happens a lot even when I least expect it).

When I finished, he began to tell me he was also from Ohio and how him and his family had moved about a year ago, how he drove trucks for a living as well and was looking to start his own business. He said my testimony really helped him and he was thankful we met.

Look at God! Even in the midst of a problem or situation I was having God was using it to have me witness someone else. He was using what looked like opposition as an opportunity. Isn't it just like God? Had I not needed the tow I wouldn't have gotten a chance to witness the driver. He needed to hear my testimony so he could be encouraged.

Needless to say; even though I didn't like what had happened to me I began to be grateful as I know better now. I can see when God is up to something. Experience is the best teacher. After arriving at the shop to drop off my car I let the driver know I was an author and had written a book about my testimony, so I shared all the info with him. He thanked me again and went on his way. I then called for an Uber so I could get home.

The next day, first thing Monday morning I started working from home as most of the world had been anyway thanks to Covid-19, but also called the repair shop to talk to the manager about my car. He said he would check it out and call me later.

After working the full day at home, the shop manager called me around 5:30pm that evening. He told me what's wrong with the car, but for some reason it didn't line up with what I saw the evening before. I asked him about the Drive Train Malfunction and Low Oil messages I had told him about earlier, but he said he didn't see that.

"Are you looking at the BMW? He said "Yes." He then said, "Well I'll take it for a drive in the morning and give you a call."

I then said "ok" and we hung up. I thought it was odd but let it go and waited for his call. The next day on what was now Tuesday morning, the shop manager called me, but I was on a work call, so he left me a message.

"Your car is fixed and ready to go, so come pick it up today." Wait... what? I didn't even get an estimate of what was wrong. I called him back and asked,

"Did you check out what I said was wrong?"

"I didn't see those things wrong," he said. I was dumbfounded.

"Waits are we talking about the same car?"

He then said, "What car are you talking about?"

Now I was downright nervous, and explained, "The white BMW SUV. The one you've worked on for me before."

The next words out of his mouth were, "I don't see that car."

"Say what? What do you mean you don't see it? I dropped it off there Sunday and we just talked about it yesterday."

"I don't see that car anywhere on my lot," he said.

"Are you sure?"

"Yes, I'm sure, I'm not lying to you."

"Ok I'm on my way up now."

Just Believe, Don't Perform

Chapter Fourteen:

"DUDE, Where is My Car"

I called for an Uber and went up to the repair shop. As soon as I got out of the Uber and was about to walk in, the manager came out and waved for me to come inside his office. Next thing I see is video on his security camera telling me that my car was in fact stolen off of the lot at 5:50 am the very next morning after I had left it.

How crazy is that?! Two thieves were able to get in and drove off with the car because my mistake was, I left the key in the car instead of putting it in the drop box for the manager to get it the next day. Also, turns out the car he was talking about initially when we were on the phone was someone's gray BMW sedan.

I then called the local Anaheim police and they told me to come in and file a report. I had also called my friend Bas as he was listed as the owner, so he came up to the shop and he took me so I could file the report. Now let me remind you, all of this is going on while I just found out I'm being hired as an employee at the company I've been working for and on top of that I'm getting a new car from them. Crazy, but that's God!

From about the time, I found out I was going to be an employee it was an extremely busy 3 weeks from the last week of July to around mid-August. Five days after the car was stolen it was found by the Anaheim police in a lot somewhere in the neighborhood from where it was stolen. Now I had to work with my insurance on the claim I had filed to have the car picked up and inspected for an estimate of damages.

The only thing noticeable was that they trashed the inside of the car, but there were no outside physical damages. There were some issues found mechanically with the car, but thanks be to God my insurance took care of everything including a nice rental car I got to drive for 30 days, so even more than what I thought they would. Talk about the favor or grace of God.

While this was all going on, I was also working with my employer that I was contracted with on off-boarding from them and at the same time working with the car company to be on-boarded with them. I was also asked to do a TV interview and 2 online interviews for my last book "Amazing Grace" as part of promotion for it. I felt at this time things were moving into a new position or season for me and even though things didn't feel very comfortable during this time because of so much going on I knew God was getting me ready for greater things. Once again, it just took trusting his timing.

Once all the car repairs were done, I gave the BMW back to my friend Bas, who sold it to me since at the time they finished I was now on-boarded as an employee for the company and now got to order my brand-new car. Because it had to be ordered and can take up to 3 months to arrive, they provided me a courtesy or loaner until the new one arrived.

Even this was a brand-new car, and I would have been satisfied if they said I had to keep it. With each event that happens I just can't help but think back to where everything started with my last book, "Amazing Grace." Who knew I would come so far from being homeless in Long Beach to making a lot of new friends and connections as well a whole new church family, now having a stable job with steady income, and driving nice new cars all the time! No way my performance merited all this as I know I made mistakes along the way, but this is all part of God's goodness and me just believing in him and his word.

Chapter Fifteen

Elevated by God

One example in the bible where things like this took place was in the book of Genesis chapter 39, where a man named Joseph was sold into slavery by his own brothers and while in an Egyptian market with spectators around was about to be purchased by a man named Potiphar, the story goes something like this.

"Now Joseph had been taken down to Egypt. And Potiphar, an officer of Pharaoh, captain of the guard, an Egyptian, brought him

from the Ishmaelites who had taken him down

there. The Lord was with Joseph, and he was a

successful man; and he was in the house of his

master the Egyptian."

Did you see that? God called Joseph a

successful man. Not because he was a slave but

because the Lord was with him. This man

literally had nothing materially, but at the same

time he had everything because the Lord was

with him. What God was and still is showing me

is that material things don't make you a success,

being with him does. We need to learn to stop

pursuing things and start pursuing HIM.

Remember Matthew 6:33 "See ye first the kingdom of God and his righteousness and all things will be added unto you. God sees our relationship with him as the only thing we really need for success in life.

Continuing with the story in Genesis 39, Potiphar would see that the Lord was with him. Verse 3 says "And his master [Potiphar] saw the Lord was with him [Joseph] and that the Lord made all he did to prosper in his hand." If you read later in Genesis chapter 41: this same man Joseph ends up being so favored and full of wisdom, he eventually became king of Egypt (verses 38 to 43) and this was even after he had been thrown in prison for being falsely accused of coming on to Potiphar's wife when she had actually come on to him! For this story read Genesis 39: 7 -23. This powerful statement offers a promise, if you can believe in God for everything in your life you will see results and good things will happen. You will become blessed enough to be a blessing to someone else.

Some of you may be thinking, "oh no… things like this would never happen to me, I mess up too much or all the time. God would never be this good to me, my works can never be good enough, God is probably always mad at me." Let me show you where a true example of the grace of God is and why you can believe in it.

The bible shows this in Luke Chapter 18. Jesus tells a story of a Pharisee and a tax collector who went to church to pray. It goes like this:

"Two men went up to the temple to pray, the one a Pharisee and the other a tax collector. The Pharisee stood and began praying to himself [in a self-righteous way] saying; God, I thank you that I'm not like the rest of men- swindlers, unjust (dishonest), adulterers or even like this tax collector. I fast twice a week, I pay tithes of all I get. But the tax collector, standing at a distance would not even raise his eyes

toward heaven, but was striking his chest [in humility and repentance] saying, God be merciful and gracious to me the sinner [that I am]. I tell you. Jesus then says, this man went to his home justified [forgiven of the guilt of sin and placed in right standing with God] rather than the other man; for anyone who exalts himself will be humbled, but he who humbles himself [forsaking self-righteous pride] will be exalted."

Chapter Sixteen:

The Grace of God

The message here is you are not too far off for him. You can receive his grace, receive his goodness, no matter what you've done. Romans 2:4 says, "it's the GOODNESS of God that leads a man to repentance."

What does repentance mean? To change your mind about something. Many people think it means "I'm sorry," but you can be sorry for something over and over and over again, it doesn't mean you've repented. To repent means you can turn around and go the other way, do a 180-degree turn. If you've messed up in life just turn it over to him, don't sit there and continue to be under condemnation or be down on yourself. Repent and receive his grace, receive his goodness. Jesus died and did it for you!

Now I want to briefly explain Matthew 6:33 which I've brought up several times, but I want to go back a few versus to verse 25 through 34 of this chapter. Jesus is teaching and he states the following.

"Therefore; I tell you, stop being worried or anxious (perpetually uneasy, distracted) about your life, as to what you will eat or what you will drink; nor about your body, as to what you will wear. Is life not more than food, and the

body more than clothing? Look at the birds of the air; they neither sow [seed] nor reap [the harvest] nor gather [crops] into barns, and yet your heavenly Father keeps feeding them. Are you not worth much more than they? And who of you by worrying can add one hour to [the length of] his life? And why are you worried about clothes? See how the lilies and wildflowers of the field grow; they do not labor, nor do they spin [wool to make clothing] yet I say to you that even as Solomon in all of his glory and splendor dressed himself like one of these. But if God so clothes the grass of the field, which is alive and green today and tomorrow is [cut and] thrown [as fuel] into the furnace, will

Just Believe, Don't Perform

HE not much more clothe you? You of little faith!

Therefore, do not worry or be anxious (perpetually uneasy, distracted), saying, what are we going to eat?' or 'What are we going to drink?' or What are we going to wear?' For the pagen [Gentiles] eagerly seek all these things; [but do not worry,] for your heavenly Father knows that you need them. But first and more importantly seek (aim at, strive after) His Kingdom and His righteousness [His way of doing and being right-the attitude and character of God], and all these things will be given to you also. So, do not worry about tomorrow; for tomorrow will worry about itself. Each day has enough trouble of its ow

Chapter Seventeen:

Getting to Know God

Where is Jesus teaching us here? Seek him *first* for everything in your life. In order to seek him you first have to get to know him. How willing will you be to seek someone or anyone you don't know?

This is what I call being "intentional" about your walk with God and your walk of faith. The more you get to know him and what he has promised in his word, the easier it will be to go to him for not only what you need in life but for anything in your life. He wants to have a relationship with you. He wants you to talk to him about not just big things but little things as well. Whatever means something to you means something to him, but you have to believe it.

Is there a scripture that backs up what I'm saying? Absolutely. Psalms 138:8 says, *"The Lord will perfect that which concerns me."* No matter what it is, God has the answers for every area of your life. It's up to you to choose to seek him for it. Once you do though, whatever you need will start showing up.

You'll run into the right people at just the right time. You'll make the right connections, get the right job, have the needed transportation, have the right amount of money, or if the money isn't there, favors. No matter what, it will all be there for you. God will begin to lead you just like a GPS navigation system in a car. And guess what? Just like that GPS in a car he won't beat you up or put you down when you miss it, mess up or go the wrong way. GPS just tells you "Re-routing, re-routing" when you make the wrong turn or miss the exit. God will just say "just repent and turn around, go this way, come over here." All through his word! That's called Amazing Grace!

Just Believe, Don't Perform

Chapter Eighteen:

The Blessings of Abraham

One thing I mentioned in my last book *Amazing Grace* that I want to elaborate on here is what is called the Blessing of Abraham from the bible. In the book of Galatians Chapter 3:29 it states, "If you are in Christ (confess and belong to Jesus), then you are Abraham's seed, and heirs accordingly to the promise." God's blessings are part of our relationship as well as inheritance under the covenant of grace which Jesus died to give us.

Just Believe, Don't Perform

The word of God tells us in Galatians 3:13-14 that "Christ has redeemed us from the curse of the law (the law of Moses from Exodus Chapter 20), becoming a curse for us so that the Blessing of Abraham might come on the Gentiles (non-Jews) in Christ Jesus, that we might receive the promise of the Spirit through faith."

It's interesting that the scripture is very specific in mentioning that Christ became a curse for us on the cross, so that we can experience and enjoy the blessing of Abraham. Who qualifies to receive this blessing? Those who are in Christ. So, receive Jesus, receive the blessing. What is the blessing? It's an empowerment to prosper in any and every area of your life. This speaks to something good. It speaks of an inheritance that you don't work for, but you can **believe** for. It happens not because of what you do but because of **whose** you are.

As a new covenant believer in Jesus, by receiving him you now belong to him, and you have a blood bought inheritance in Christ as the seed. You are an heir, the heir according to the promise. This promise is found in Romans 4:13 where it is said "For the promise that he would be the heir of the world was not to Abraham or his seed through the law, but through the righteousness of faith."

Just Believe, Don't Perform

To break this down even further the word "world" here in the original Greek text of the word means *kosmos* which means you are an heir to a whole circle of earthly goods, endowments, riches, advantages, and pleasures all through Christ and his finished work on the cross. Now I'll say it in modern language, because you are an heir in Christ you have a right to whatever it is you need in life. The key is you have access by grace (unmerited favor) through faith. Faith is and always will be the key to this, as it goes on to say in Romans 4:14 "For if those who depend on the law (of Moses) are heirs, their faith is made void (means nothing) and the promise is of no effect."

I truly believe my study and meditation of these scriptures are some of the keys to what has not only helped me get through trying and difficult times but has propelled me into a position to write books like this. Now my desire is to pass along this information so others can be blessed as well. Knowledge is power and what is more powerful than the word of God. This is the ability to get results and become successful in every area of life.

One thing that's very apparent is that God uses people all day and every day. He uses people with willing hearts, he uses people of all races, genders and regardless of religion or political party. He uses people even when they don't realize they are being used, but those who are surrendered to his will for their life will know. Coming from my hometown in Columbus, Ohio, I knew a lot of people, made a lot of friends, and connected with many others but in moving to California, the number of friends and connections I've made in 5 years of being here has amazed me.

In the book of Psalms 37:23 it states, "The steps of a good man are ordered by the Lord: and he delights in his way." When walking by faith and relying on Him to lead you he will place people in your path that will be designed to help you, befriend you, keep you company when needed, or build relationships that can lead to other friendships and opportunities that will contribute to your success. God will always use people.

He's using me to speak to you and as you've seen in these books, he's used others to bless me. I can never predict how it happens or with whom but once it does, I know it was from him and it always happens at the right time, not always on our time but always on time.

I think back to the friendships I've had since high school. My friend Mike who I've known and been the tightest with since our high school days. My friend Dwayne who I met around 2005 and has always been there as well. Other friends like Kevin, Scott, Richie who I also met in high school. Troy G, Chris, Doug, Terry, and John who I all met through Dwayne. All from my hometown, all played pivotal parts in my friendship with them even when they didn't realize it.

I talked about my friend Mark who God used strongly in helping confirm that I was on the right path in taking the move to California. There were others as well, like my friends Kay and her husband Todd. I met Kay while working on a previous job and would always see her at the gym. She was encouraging and always gave me good advice. There were also friends like Lorna, Michelle, and Huda who really helped me realize my gift whether they knew it or not. I didn't even realize it at the time, but I do now.

Then I moved to California in 2017, and even while dealing with homelessness doors were opening for me to meet people. In my book Amazing Grace, I talked about meeting my friend Rebecca at the restaurant in Long Beach who ended giving me my first car. She also introduced me to the beginning of my social life in Long Beach that year by meeting my friends Kelly and Shannon along with a whole crew of folks while she was also working part time within Belmont Shore in Long Beach.

Just Believe, Don't Perform

Kelly is someone I became instant friends with, and it was a Godsend to meet them when I did. I was staying at the homeless shelter when we met, but they didn't judge or treat me any differently, they accepted me right away. There's of course Shannon and my Beacon for Him family as well which I've mentioned. The most amazing thing was meeting my friend Ebony who was the cousin of my friend Dwayne from Ohio.

The chance birthday dinner at which I ended up meeting Derek, also from Ohio, and Kiran who I would end up becoming roommates 2 years after meeting him. Finding out Derek and I knew so many people back home, but we had never met until here in California still gets me to this day.

Then after getting let go from my previous job and landing a job at a car company in Irvine which then led to meeting so many more new people is astonishing. I would not say I have as many friends here in Cali as I do back in Ohio but with as many as I've met it sure feels that way. Then there was meeting my friend Dawn, also through Dwayne, which was right on time as well. Being able to spend one year at Christmas time with her and her family when I couldn't go to Ohio was just what was needed to help me get through another transition.

Just Believe, Don't Perform

I also spent Thanksgiving my first year in Cali with Dwayne's other cousin David and his family, then the next year with a lady, also employed by the same company I work for, named Ms. Judy who hosted all of us in Ohio transplants and some others for Thanksgiving. Through meeting Ebony, Derek, and Kiran that initial night of her birthday I met so many other people such as Byron and Kari, who are married, Mike and Amy, also married, Mimi and Tonya, among so many other friends I met through them. There are also many other connections and friends I have made through my employer (too many to name).

The point of all this is to re-emphasize how God uses people and situations to bless us and bring people together. I would not have gotten through difficult times without these people.

Just Believe, Don't Perform

Chapter Nineteen:

Five Key Principles

I want to take this last chapter to go through what I feel are a few key points or principles that can be used on your journey or walk of faith. These 5 key points can help you in your walk as God leads you into purpose and will establish his word as the foundation for you. Here they are as follows:

• Know God loves you – In the book of John Chapter 17:22 and 23 Jesus is praying to the father and says these words; *"I have given to them the glory and honor which You have given*

Me, that they may be one, just as We are one; I in them and You in me, that they may be perfected and completed into one, so that the world may know [without any doubt] that you sent me, and [that you] have loved them, just as You have loved Me."

When you know someone truly loves you it empowers you and you feel as though you can do almost anything. That's how our heavenly father wants us to feel as his children, like we can do anything through HIM.

In Mark 9:23 Jesus states *"If you can believe, all things are possible to them who believes."* Yet again the key is to believe. I have found focusing more on God's love for me than my love for him has propelled me further than anything else. Even when I mess up, which happens often, it never changes how God feels about me because I know he loves me like I'm his own son. This is powerful.

• Know that you are the righteousness of God in Christ – Knowing your identity could be the difference in succeeding or failing in life. While God's promise is to love us no matter what, we still have to take responsibility to know it.

2 Corinthians 5:21 states *"God made him (Jesus) who knew no sin to be sin for us, so that in him we would become the righteousness of God."* When you know who you are in Christ you won't be inclined to believe claims from the

enemy or anyone else. You also re-establish yourself in his word, which is something you need to do daily in order to experience good success.

Whether you use daily devotionals or just pull-out scripture on your own, it will give you confidence in his word working for you no matter what situation you find yourself in. It will help you get out or through it, but you need to be and here's a key word, "intentional" about seeking him. Remember it's not who you are but "whose" you are as a child of God.

● Know that there's power in your words – As I stated before scripture tells us in Proverbs

18:21 *"Life and Death are in the power of the tongue."* Proverbs 6:2 also says, *"You are snared by the words of your mouth."* Think about it, you use your mouth for just about everything. You tell people when you feel good or bad, you are interviewed and get a job, get married, to tell someone how you feel about them, to give direction, in authority, on and on and on.

Even God created the heavens and earth by what, His words! Read the beginning book of Genesis, Chapter 1. Everything God created was words so the same goes for you and me. If I tell someone I love them, I'll get a reaction and if I tell someone I hate them I'll get another reaction. Words can make love or war depending on who you are talking to and your relationship with them.

I once heard Lisa Marie Presley, daughter of Elvis and once the wife of Michael Jackson, say in an interview shortly after Michael Jackson died, that he used to tell her he would be dead by the time he was 50. Guess when he died. In 2009 when he was 49. There are many other examples, but you can't tell me words don't have power. Why not use the word of God to your advantage as power and success for your life?

• Know you have the ability to give - Whether it is your time or your money, being a giver is one of the greatest feelings ever, especially when it's done with the right heart and intent. I personally love to give and not expect anything in return. In the scripture, Matthew 25: 40 Jesus said about those who were hungry, thirsty, in need of clothes or sick, *"whatever you did for one of the least of these brothers and sisters of mine, you did it for me."*

When I was homeless and had very little after losing the job that brought me to California, it meant everything to be led to a ministry outreach that served people who had been in less fortunate circumstances. It took all the focus off myself and any of my works and put it all on doing the work of helping others, all the while believing God was taking care of me. I truly was walking by faith and not by sight where my life was concerned, and while it didn't feel good at first; when I saw how some people received what I could give I loved it.

Even at the homeless shelter to be able to give back or share knowledge of God's word was extremely powerful. One conversation or act of kindness was the difference in someone going down the right path or potentially a wrong one. I realized the truth in Acts 20:35 in scripture where it states it's truly *"more blessed to give than to receive."*

- Be Thankful – I'm a huge believer that attitude determines your altitude. The scripture says in Philippians 4: 6, "*Do not be anxious about anything, but in every situation, by prayer and petition, with thanksgiving, let your requests be made known to God.*" Truth be told God does not want us to worry, be stressed or anxious all the time as that hinders us from walking by faith.

Complaining also does not move us into the faith he wants us to walk in either. He knows we have challenges in this world, but he wants us to bring our cares and concerns to him with thanksgiving because he knows he has the answers already there for us. He wants us to rest in him and what he's done for us (Matthew 11:28 and Hebrews 4:11). Give God purposeful thanks and remember he already not only knows your situation; he also knows your destination, just like that GPS in a car. You don't ever have to lose a battle that he's already won for you through his word.

Lastly, I can't finish this book without extending an invitation to anyone who may have never received Christ as Savior and Lord. Romans 10: 9-10 states *"If you declare with your mouth, 'Jesus is Lord,' and believe in your heart that God raised him from the dead, you will be saved. For it is with the heart that you believe and are justified, and it is with your mouth that you profess your faith and are saved."*

If you have never done this and know you need him in your life, it is easy. Just say something like, "Lord, I'm a sinner in need of a savior. I believe in what Jesus did at the cross for me, I believe he died for my sins. Come into my life, I accept you, believe you, and confess you now as lord over my life. Thank you Jesus I'm saved."

Now go find a church, ministry outreach, small group, or organization that can help educate you, build your faith, and walk in his promises for your life. And here is great news for you as you're walking by faith. 2 Corinthians 1: 20 God says his promises are "Yes and Amen." Even when you mess up (and you will) 2 Timothy 2:13 says "If we are unfaithful, he remains faithful for he cannot deny himself." Remember as you're walking whatever doesn't make sense makes FAITH so **Just Believe, Don't Perform!**

Acknowledgments

To my Parents. Robert and JoAnne Barnes: Thank you for being what parents should be and making it easy to honor you. Thank you for your prayers, loving me unconditionally and bringing both a holy fear of reverence and faith into our relationship which helped me grow into who I am as a man. I couldn't ask for better people to call my mom and dad. God has truly blessed me. Love you for life.

To my brothers, Lee Barnes, and Robert Cauley: Thank you for your support. I know we don't talk all the time, but I feel your love, prayers and support as brothers. I appreciate you both more than you know especially being there for the family as I moved out of state. Love you to life as well.

Special thanks to my Sister-In-Law Felicia Cauley. Thank you for your continuing help and support in the writing process and inspiring me to put this content out there. I appreciate your knowledge and support as I could not have done this without you. Love you sis.

I want to lastly say a super, super huge **THANK YOU** to anyone and everyone who has had anything to do with being in this thing called life with me and inspiring me through this journey. To all family, friends, coworkers to acquaintances, and even just random people I've met from Ohio to California and anywhere in between. There are way too many names of people to thank but just know God used you whether you realized it or not, especially the ones who came along at pivotal times in this journey along with writing this book. I would not be where I am today without you, your support, and your prayers. Many thanks to all the churches, nonprofit and faith-based organizations that allowed me to exercise my faith and serve in the communities both in Ohio and California. My prayer for you is that the Lord blesses you, keep you, may his face shine on you, and be gracious to you all!

Troy Barnes lives in Southern California and works as an IT Professional spanning over 20 years, 10 as a certified IT Asset Management professional, working for various companies. Troy is passionate about helping and serving others as he has given his time and resources to various churches and organizations both in Ohio and California. He is continuously growing in his life journey seeking God's overall plan for his life. Troy stays active by working out, volunteering, some travel and spending time with friends, family. Just Believe, Don't Perform is his second book. His first book Amazing Grace "My Journey into God's Unmerited Favor" was released in October 2020. You can follow him on Facebook, LinkedIn (Troy Barnes) and Instagram (tbarnes2432) as well email him at tbarnes2432@gmail.com